IMAGES
of America

African-American Education in
WESTMORELAND
COUNTY

Cassandra Burton
1999

The following is a basic architectural description of a simple A-frame, or log cabin, one-room schoolhouse. These buildings are located many times in churches or on someone's home, farm, or property where children lived. The interior design consisted of wooden benches and/or desks; a pot-belly stove, usually in the middle of the floor space; wooden floors; a platform, upon which the teacher stood; hooks on the walls to hang coats (many times, the girls used the right side and the boys, the left); a blackboard; no indoor running water; and no indoor restrooms.

For the first schools, building costs were the responsibility of the community; thus, they varied in size and style. We do know that the older field schools were built in 1813 at a cost of $15 to $20 for a modest one-room cabin. By January 1928, a 5-by-6 outhouse would cost around $27, and repairs on an existing outhouse would cost $14. Construction of these one-room structures was done by the men who had built the grand plantation homes.

Cassandra Burton

Copyright © 1999 by Cassandra Burton.
ISBN 0-7385-0145-X

Published by Arcadia Publishing,
an imprint of Tempus Publishing, Inc.
2 Cumberland Street
Charleston, SC 29401

Printed in Great Britain.

Library of Congress Catalog Card Number: Applied for.

For all general information contact Arcadia Publishing at:
Telephone 843-853-2070
Fax 843-853-0044
E-Mail arcadia@charleston.net

For customer service and orders:
Toll-Free 1-888-313-BOOK

Visit us on the internet at http://www.arcadiaimages.com

In Westmoreland County, all our native sons are important, whether a descendant of Robert E. Lee of Stratford or Israel Jones of Springfield Farm in Sandy Point. Education was and continues to be important to all who live here.

Contents

Acknowledgments		6
Introduction		7
1.	Washington District	11
2.	Montross School District	29
3.	Cople School District	57
4.	Rosenwald Schools	95
5.	Typical School Days: Teachers and Lesson Plans	107

Acknowledgments

The author would like to thank all who spent hours looking for old photos and allowing me into their homes to spend hours searching through old papers and photo albums. The taping of priceless oral histories and memories of the schools that are now gone and of the people's youth aided greatly in putting this book together. To the following families, I am especially appreciative: Johnson, Payne, Wilson, Smith, Roberts, Ware, Hoban, Cooper, Jenkins, Lowe, Weldon, Fisher, Richards, Gordon, Lee, Jones, Brown, Green, Roane, Reed, Willis, Hoban, Campbell, Newton, Brown, Green, Nickens, Dudley, Pierce, Hall, Ashton, Clayton, Tate, Gaskins, Ball, Hughes, Price, Henry, Crabbe, Lucas, Streets, Philpot, Harris, and Reverend W.T. Morris.

A special thanks goes to the following: Martha Jenkins Roane, who was the first to come forward to help; her son, Calvin Jenkins, who continued after her; Sherman Tate; Gladys Johnson; Edna Hazel Newton Crabbe, who pushed me on; and my extra hands, Lois Johnson, Melanie Hall, Adele Roane, and Lucille Ware, who were always there for me.

I would also like to thank the ministers of the Westmoreland County, especially Reverend William B. Scott, Reverend Henry Lee, and Reverend Frank Coleman, for their aid in securing the forgotten history of the one- and two-room schoolhouses.

I am deeply appreciative of the total support for this book from the following: the Library of Virginia and its staff; the A.T. Johnson Alumni Association; the Westmoreland County Branch of the NAACP; the Westmoreland County School Board; our wonderful superintendent of schools, Dr. Larry Hixson; and his assistant, Mr. George Ortman.

This, my first book, is dedicated to my husband, Malachi Burton, and our wonderful children and grandchildren, whose love and support enabled me to spend countless hours researching and interviewing. Everyone's history is important and only when you know from where you've come can you appreciate where you are. May the children of yesterday, today, and tomorrow of all races treasure the education they receive today.

Introduction

Forbidden by law and unable to read or write, African Americans passed their history down through songs, stories, and poems. The Negro mind was highly trained to memorize.

In 1865, when Westmoreland County's native son Robert E. Lee of Stratford Hall Plantation surrendered to Ulysses S. Grant at Appomattox Court House, 4 million slaves would suddenly gain their freedom—200,000 in Virginia alone!

Following the war, during the period known as Reconstruction, African Americans were encouraged by the Freedman's Bureau to establish their own churches and schools. In Westmoreland County, white churches often aided the "colored" members who had attended the white church with their prior owner to set up their own church on adjacent ground.

As Harrison I. Smith so well stated in his memoirs, "The church is the mightiest agency on earth for the regulation of human progress, the ally of all true reforms, it is the sublime character making institution of the world; it relates mankind to God and to one another in a happy and useful fellowship."

Having observed firsthand the value placed on education by the white population, blacks sought educational opportunities for their children. Schools were often set up in these churches, with the benches being used Monday through Friday for the education of the children. It was not unusual for the minister to be the teacher, which had been the case in Episcopal churches for centuries. As far back as 1724, the Washington Parish Episcopal Church in Oak Grove, Virginia, reported to the bishop in London on the status of what was being done for "public schooling" for the youth.

During antebellum times, it was illegal in Virginia to educate blacks; for example, a Norfolk woman was prosecuted in 1854 for teaching a free African-American boy to read and write and was jailed for 30 days. Fortunately, this never occurred in Westmoreland County. Isolated incidents have occurred in the county prior to 1870 of a few free blacks and slaves being able to read and write. Who actually taught them will forever remain a mystery, although the question has been raised whether a slave sitting in on the teaching sessions of a young owner's son absorbed all that was taught or did the lady of the house provide instruction for a few?

On January 30, 1813, Virginia created "the Poor School Society," which allowed whites to attend these small one-room schoolhouses, commonly referred to as "Old Field Schools." However, no person of color was allowed to attend these schools, which cost only $15 to $20 to build. In 1870, statistics showed that only 10% of blacks were getting some type of education. The illiteracy rate for blacks was put at 79.9%, as opposed to 50% for whites.

In 1870 the first state superintendent of schools, William H. Ruffner, was the author of an act to establish and maintain a uniform system of "Public Free Schools"; its most important

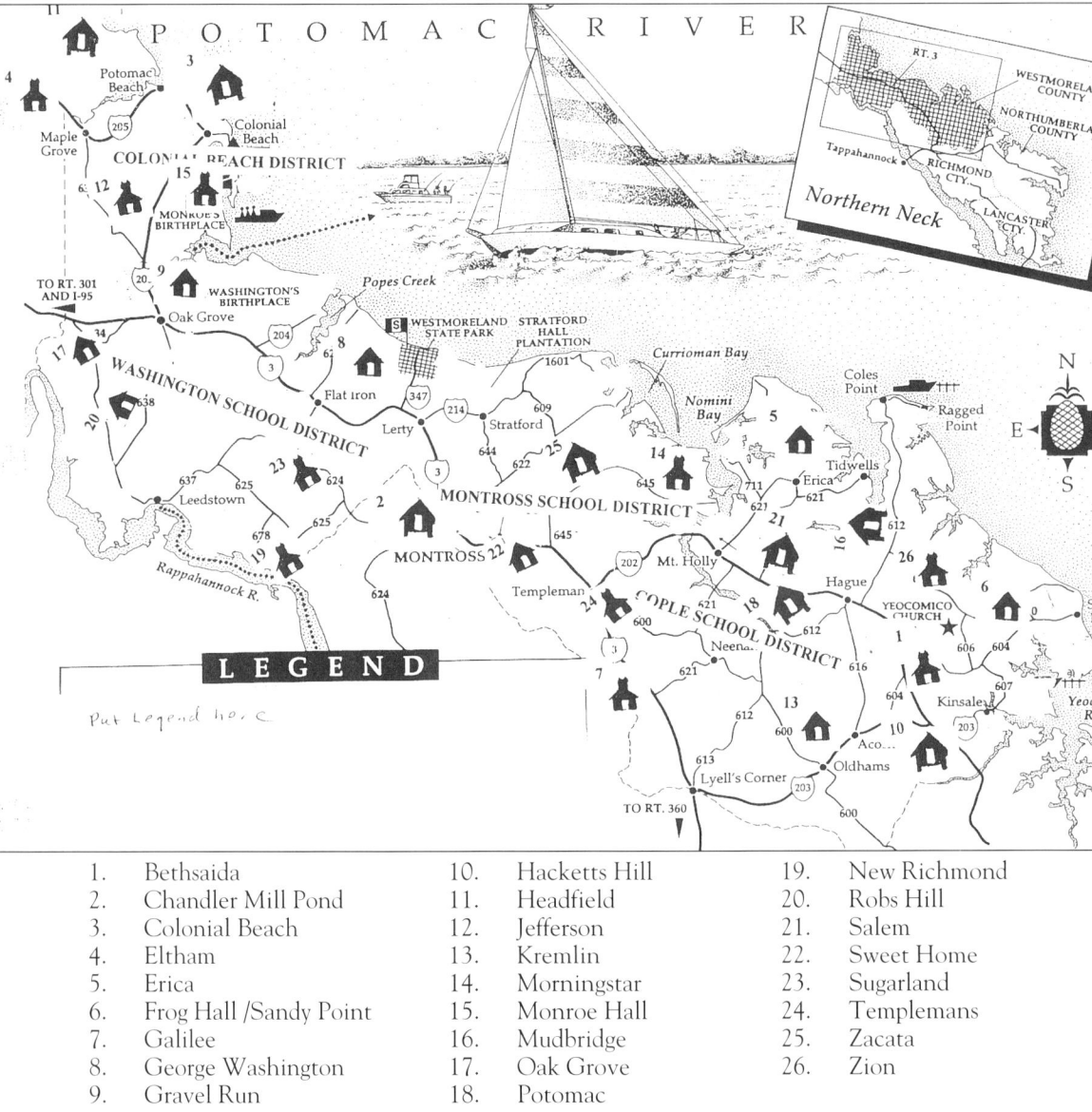

1.	Bethsaida	10.	Hacketts Hill	19.	New Richmond
2.	Chandler Mill Pond	11.	Headfield	20.	Robs Hill
3.	Colonial Beach	12.	Jefferson	21.	Salem
4.	Eltham	13.	Kremlin	22.	Sweet Home
5.	Erica	14.	Morningstar	23.	Sugarland
6.	Frog Hall /Sandy Point	15.	Monroe Hall	24.	Templemans
7.	Galilee	16.	Mudbridge	25.	Zacata
8.	George Washington	17.	Oak Grove	26.	Zion
9.	Gravel Run	18.	Potomac		

provision read as follows: "The public free schools shall be free to all persons between the ages of five and twenty-one years residing within a school district, provided that white and colored persons shall not be taught in the same schools, but in separate schools, under the same regulations as to management, usefulness, and efficiency." With the exception of the segregation clause, Ruffner's bill of 1870 was the true origin of public education as we know it today.

Education throughout the South was aided by some wealthy Northerners. In 1867 to benefit the destitute areas of the South, George Peabody established the first educational philanthropy in the United States with a gift of $2 million. A highly successful Massachusetts merchant, he believed it was the duty of the wealthier portions of our nation to assist those less fortunate. His only stipulation was that the money be used for elementary education of the common people.

The Peabody Fund was administered by a general agent who traveled to schools throughout the South. The agent was responsible for addressing state legislatures to advocate for a "free public school system." Funds could not be given where discrimination occurred—perhaps that is why in 1870, Virginia created a "separate but equal" school system because funds had to be used for the education of both races. The Peabody Fund existed until 1914, when it turned its remaining funds over to the Slater Fund. Both black and white schools of Westmoreland County benefited from the Peabody Fund between 1870 and 1914.

The Slater Fund was started with a million-dollar gift in 1882 as the first philanthropy in America devoted to the education of the African American. Slater was a wealthy Connecticut textile manufacturer. While inspired by the work of the George Peabody Fund, he was specific in stating that his fund be used exclusively for the uplifting of the largely emancipated population of the South by conferring on them the blessings of a Christian education. The Slater Fund set the precedence for public reporting by foundations, requiring his trustees to distribute each year a printed description of their work to the Library of Congress and to state libraries. Westmoreland County is indebted to the funds we received, especially toward the building of our A.T. Johnson High School in 1937.

In 1902, John D. Rockefeller funded his "GEB," or General Education Board, because he felt the first efforts must be toward improvements of economic conditions in the South before education could develop there. School systems, he believed, could not just be given to persons of the South because they were not prosperous enough to support themselves. The board decided it must first teach the farmer how to farm. Its next venture was to devote itself to aiding communities by providing educational facilities. Westmoreland County benefited from these funds, with the white schools receiving help first and black schools receiving aid in 1910.

In 1907 a Quaker and Philadelphia philanthropist named Anna T. Jeanes donated $1 million to be used for the rudimentary education of Southern blacks. With the establishment of the Negro Rural School Fund, she entrusted the money to Booker T. Washington of the Tuskegee Institute and Hollis Burke Frissell of the Hampton Institute to maintain and assist rural schools for blacks in the South. The fund was commonly referred to as the "Jeanes Fund." The purpose of the fund initially supported "industrial teachers," who traveled from rural school to rural school teaching sewing, canning, basketry, and woodworking. These skills were thought to be a practical way to improve rural education. Jeanes teachers were master teachers, or called supervisors, and they were a valuable part of Westmoreland County's educational process for black youth. Jeanes teachers were encouraged to continue their education, for by the mid-1940s, 15% of these teachers held masters-level degrees. Gradually the salaries of the Jeanes teachers were taken over by the county. The Homemakers Clubs introduced by the Jeanes teachers later became the federal government's Home Demonstration program.

The Odd Fellows were called the Grand United Order of Odd Fellows, a secular group that followed the principles started in seventeenth-century England and established in America by Thomas Wiley in Baltimore. Because of the close water connection between Baltimore and Westmoreland County, this idea flowed quickly into the area. The Odd Fellows built lodges for their meetings and stored supplies needed in the burial of their dead. The members of this group would serve as the volunteers that not only visited the sick, but transported and prepared for burial of dead persons in the county. Several Odd fellow halls have been used as classroom space for the children of Westmoreland County.

Federal funds, both state and county, the Colored School Leagues, and citizens' contributions have all aided in the education of the Westmoreland County of yesteryear. Roads were poor, and transportation was simple in this rural community, meaning schools developed in the clusters where people lived. Pennies were often collected in the community to pay a teacher's salary, and teachers often boarded with families. Persons from one community seldom came in contact with each other. Teachers throughout their careers taught at many different schools.

Westmoreland County's Black Schoolhouses
1870–1958
(alphabetical listing)

1. Bethsaida
2. First Chandler Hill Pond
3. Second Chandler Mill Pond
4. First Colonial Beach
5. Second Colonial Beach
6. Eltham
7. First Erica
8. Second Erica
9. First Frog Hall
10. Second Frog Hall / Sandy Point
11. Frog Hall / Sandy Point Chapel
12. First Galilee
13. Second Galilee in Odd Fellows Hall
14. George Washington
15. Gravel Run
16. First Hacketts Hill
17. Second Hacketts Hill
18. Headfield
19. Jefferson
20. First Kremlin
21. Second Kremlin
22. Monroe Hall No. 6
23. Morningstar
24. First Mudbridge
25. Second Mudbridge
26. Oak Grove
27. First Potomac School (log cabin)
28. Potomac
29. New Richmond
30. Robs Hill
31. Salem
32. Sweet Home
33. Sugarland
34. Templemans
35. First Zacata
36. Second Zacata
37. Third Zacata
38. Fourth Zacata
39. First Zion
40. Second Zion
41. Zion space in the Odd Fellows Hall

One
WASHINGTON DISTRICT

COLONIAL BEACH SCHOOL. The first Colonial Beach School was a one-room schoolhouse until it was sold in 1942 to a Mr. Brown and made into a private residence.

The second Colonial Beach School moved around the corner to Lincoln Avenue when this two-room schoolhouse was completed in 1942.

Reverend Charles Payton of Morningstar Church attended Colonial Beach Elementary School, which went up to grade seven.

Mrs. Ethel Watts Lomax, remembered well by present and former Headfield students, taught at several Westmoreland County schools.

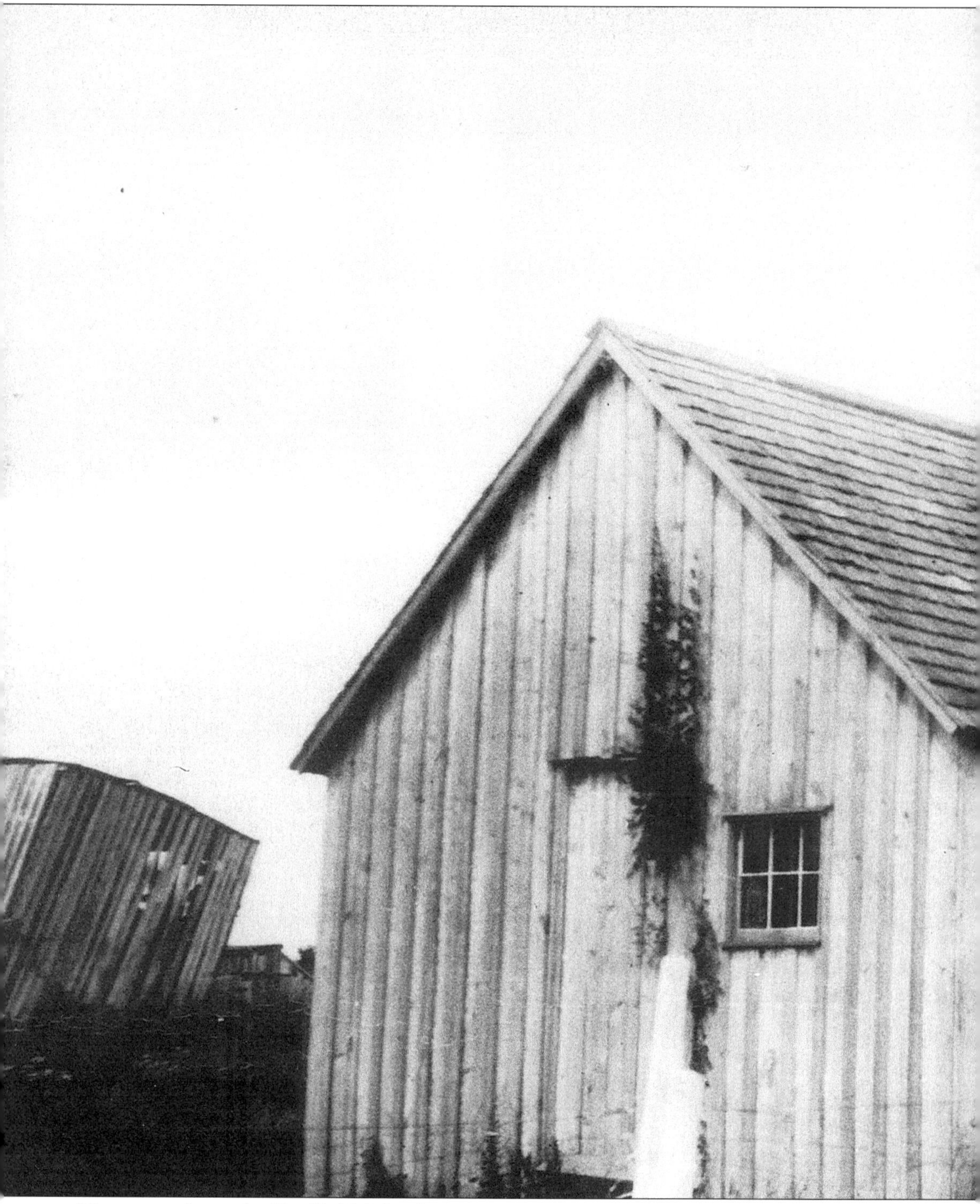

This image shows the Headfield School.

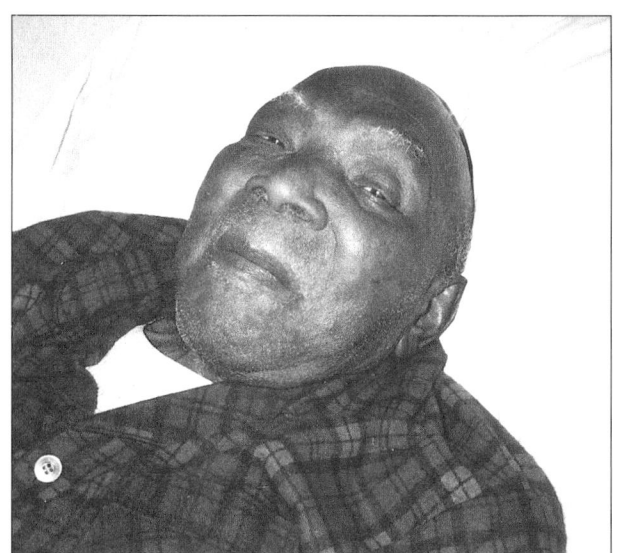

Steven Dudley, a student, was remembered well by his beloved school. Those students who attended were proud of their one-room schoolhouse, despite the fact that it was difficult to keep a teacher in such a remote and rural area. Some of these much loved teachers are Mrs. Lomax, Reverend Johnson, Miss Mary Thomas Lawson, and Mary Burnett. Unfortunately, the school was forced to close when the community could not find a replacement teacher.

Ella Watts, a former Headfield student, visits the original site of the Headfield School, now called New Monrovia Road, Colonial Beach.

Mrs. Campbell's Eltham School League Minutes give a splendid example of how God was put first and the pride citizens took in their school and concern for their country. We in Westmoreland County, Virginia, are grateful to Mrs. Campbell for the only known existing school league minutes. Organizational records give insight as to what the group is responding to and the feelings of the times.

Eltham School League Minutes

This Eltham School League Ledger was carefully kept by Mrs. Campbell (pictured on page 17).

Eltham School League Minutes
March 6, 1946
(Courtesy of Mrs. Etta Campbell Hughes)

"The Senior League met and held its regular meeting on the above date. The meeting was called to order by the President. The meeting was opened by the chaplin scripture reading and prayer by chaplin. It was properly moved and seconded that minutes of the previous meeting be read, received, and adopted.

Unfinished business was called for; the painting of the school was discussed. Motion made by Mrs. Syvetta Richards seconded by Mrs. Lillie M. Butler that Mr. Warren Campbell paint the school inside, the ceiling, and down to the windows. Miss Thomas reminded us the school grounds needed cleaning. Mr. Bushrod said he would try to get it cleaned before the next meeting on the 1st Wednesday in April.

Next was new business; Miss Thomas told the league about the notice she had received asking each family to contribute something towards the "War Fund Drive." Motion made by Mrs. Syvette Richards seconded by Mrs. Lillie M. Butler that each family contribute 50¢ to help make up the sum of $5.00 to be turned in for this purpose.

It was also announced at this meeting there would be entertainment at the school on the 19th of March.

Next was the financial roll call. Total amount of dues 80¢. It was properly moved and seconded that we adjourn."

Former teacher F.O. Robinson-Pryor, originally from Baltimore, Maryland, recalls how this one-room school had a stove in the middle of the room and desks on each side. Grades primer thru seventh were all assembled here. The curriculum consisted of reading, arithmetic, spelling, geography, language, handwriting, and civics. There were three recess periods during the day: ten minutes in the morning, noontime, and ten minutes at 2 p.m. Eltham Park was created by whitewashing tree stumps in the schoolyard. After the parents and students cleaned and trimmed the brush, the park was an enjoyable place to just sit or eat their lunch. Robinson-Pryor's children walked 2 to 3 miles to school on unpaved roads. In severe weather the roads became so muddy that some parents would keep their children home. Despite their rural setting, Eltham participated in the county-sponsored Music Festival. One year, Eltham won by singing "Ain't Dat Good News" (see page 112), a Negro spiritual lead by Virginia Richards; the prize was two storybooks.

Monroe Hall School No. 6 was a frame schoolhouse that was built in the late 1800s. According to the school board minutes of June 9, 1926, the school was to be closed at the end of the 1926–1927 school year. Teachers who taught here included Ms. Fannie Tinsley, Mrs. Noel, Mrs. Marie Richards, Mr. Hall in 1923–1924, and Mrs. Ethal Watts Lomax.

Still standing, this well-constructed schoolhouse has known better times.

Eight-year-old Raven Harris looks upon the construction and notices the light the large windows provided—of course, the building was heated with a wood stove. There was and continues to be no indoor plumbing. The mere size of the ceiling gave this old building a regal presence.

Harrison I. Smith was the president of the Washington District County School League. Many trips were made to the school board seeking greater educational opportunities for the black youth.

Before Westmoreland County had a Parent Teacher Association, the county had Colored School Leagues. Each school had their own league and duly elected officers. The league would hold monthly meetings to work for the common goal of maintaining and seeing that the black children received a proper education. Many of the early league members born prior to 1870 had been denied an educational opportunity. League members raised money and sought outside funds to add in the betterment of their schools. They petitioned the school board for buildings, more teachers, transportation for their children, educational supplies, and more schools.

The Sugarland School was a small one-room schoolhouse. Lucille Ware, who went to school there, remembers crossing a bridge everyday to get to the schoolhouse and that in the schoolhouse there was a bucket that children used to put their hard-boiled eggs in until lunchtime. Mrs. Ware can still smell that distinct odor, of which she is still not fond. Teachers at Sugarland included Ms. Viola Weldon, Mrs. Ardell Hoban, Ms. Teresa Decalender, and Ms. Mary Johnson.

School Board Minutes
June 11, 1930

William Roy asked to move Sugarland to a place near Longwood Gate. Allowed to move the schoolhouse. School board to purchase a site of 2 acres. It was decided to sell the old site.

This is a portrait of a 1930s Sugarland class, pictured with their teacher Ms. Mary Johnson. The students are, from left to right, as follows: (front row) Allen Roy, Ernest Posey, Madgeoline Haskins, Mary Anne Jackson, Floyd Davis, Mary Jessie Johnson, Leroy Haskins, Opal Ball, Frances Hunter, Florence Jackson, and Broadus Roy; (middle row) Elvin Ball, James Roy, William Johnson, Hazel Ball, Laura Jackson, and Willie Johnson; (back row) Miss Mary Johnson (teacher) and Edith Hunter.

Ardell Hoban was not only a student, but she returned as a teacher. She recalled how in the spring of 1933 Sugarland was moved from Foneswood over to William Johnson's home.

Maude Ware taught at Sugarland, as well as at a number of other schools.

School Board Minutes
October 13, 1937

"A delegation was present from Potomac Mills stating that Gravel Run School was closed and at least 20 children living within the vicinity of the school and that Sugarland had been condemned and was in a deplorable condition and suggested that we reopen Gravel Run School and transport the children from Sugarland to Gravel Run. They were told this matter would be taken up when the superintendent arrived home."

Going back to the 1870s, Gravel Run, still standing on King's Highway, was in a community known as Potomac Mills. Its present owners, Mr. and Mrs. Peyton, have meticulously restored the building with several additions: an enclosed porch on the front and additional living space added to the side and back of the home. This former two-room schoolhouse was still being used into the 1950s. Mary Johnson taught there for $75 per month back in 1923–1924.

The famous school bell that she rang daily is all that remains of the original school equipment held by her niece Susan Roberts. Other teachers who taught at the school were Carrie Johnson, Miss Maggie Simms, Minnie Byrd, and Joseph Tompkins.

This is a late 1800s schoolhouse, which sat on Robs Hill, now Leedstown Road.

This is a Robs Hill School class.

Fondly remembered by Mrs. Alberta Byrd are the following teachers: Mrs. Ella Bushrod, Miss Jones, Miss Robinson, Mrs. Heart, Mrs. Dorothy Payne, Mrs. Maggie Simms Nash, Mr. Fowler, Mrs. M.B. Richards, Miss Horcum, and an Industrial Arts teacher named Mrs. Mammie Roane.

New Richmond School, an early 1900s framed building, was located next to Grant's Hill Baptist Church. Mrs. Pattie Bankett taught here during the school year of 1937–1938, and Pauline Johnson Washington (pictured here) taught at New Richmond and down in Zacata when she roomed with the Reed family.

School Board Minutes
September 11, 1930

"A delegation of patrons from Richmond Hill neighborhood appeared before the Board and requested that the school be opened, this school having been closed by reason of small attendance. These patrons state there were now 25 children in the neighborhood and pledged their support toward getting them to school. The Board directed Mr. Newton to investigate this situation and if it were found correct as stated, to arrange for the school to reopen on October 7, 1940."

The Oak Grove Colored School was a small, one-room, wood-framed schoolhouse that has survived since the late 1800s. This school had among its many teachers the following: Ms. Maggie Simms and Gladys Bankette. With the addition of indoor plumbing, this building is used as a home today.

Jefferson School

Located in Monroe Hall area on Monroe Highway, Colonial Beach area, it was located up near Monroe Hall on a lot purchased by the Colored Patrons. L.D. was paid $200 for moving the building. (From the School Board Minutes from September 7, 1933.)

George Washington School

Located on what is now King's Highway by the telephone tower, George Washington School had been a white school. When the white children were bused to the consolidated school in Montross, the building was given to the black population in September 1926. As Reverend Lee and Lucille Ware explained after a Christmas program, this fine schoolhouse burned down. According to school board minutes, the lot was sold on October 16, 1934, for $71.50.

Two
Montross School District

The church community of Hinnom went from having just a Sunday school at the Morning Star Church to holding classes five days a week. They sent a letter to Mrs. Smith seeking her services. The school building sat to the left of the present-day church building. Only a few persons are left who remember this school. Other teachers who taught here included Ms. Lucinda Pratt and a Mrs. Johnson.

The students of the Chandler Mill Pond class, c. 1938, are as follows: (first row) Ivary Branson, Noah Branson, Herbert Johnson, Daniel Payne, Theodwell Payne, and Julian Tate; (second row) Ruby Branson, Bernice Reed, Virginia Kelly, Virginia Crawley, Katherine Branson, Natalie Payne, Catherine Branson, and Charles Edward Tate; (third row) Lloyd Branson,

Robert Reed, Annie Kelly, Sarah Payne, Ethel Tate, Iodele Payne, Ruby Reed, and Dorothy Payne (teacher); (fourth row) Charles Edward Tate, Eleanor Reed, Alma Payne, and Evelyn Tate.

Born in Farmer's Fork in Richmond County in 1885, Lula Langdon Smith graduated from Minor's Teacher's College in Washington, D.C. She taught at the Piney Grove School in Farmer's Fork in Richmond County for two years; the Morningstar School in Hinnom for four years (1916–1920); and the Salem School in Mount Holly for two years.

Pictured here are two Chandler Mill Pond students: Charles "Charlie" Johnson and his wife, Ethel Payne Johnson, who was the daughter of Westley "Wes" Payne. Wes Payne was the last of the slavechildren to leave Stratford Hall Plantation.

On October 8, 1930, a delegation from the Crookhorn community went to the Westmoreland County School Board advocating for a black school in their community. According to the records, the patrons agreed to furnish the house and fuel, and the school board would pay the teacher Mrs. Clara Selden's $40 per month salary at Sweet Home School. At times, to get a school, the citizens of a community had to pay the teacher's salary as well. While serving as a school, the gable side of the building faced the road, and the Payne family lived upstairs. By 1932, the school board was paying George Thompson to deliver three cords of wood to the school at the cost of $3.50 each.

William H. Weldon was a teacher at the Sweet Home School.

Joseph D. Reed remembered well the four Zacata schools because his father and other relatives helped to build these fine structures. He recalled how the first school was located in the early 1900s on the farm of his uncle, George Reed, who lived on Zacata Road in Zacata. Mr. Reed had the school built on his property for the education of black children. As the number of children outgrew the space limitations of the small schoolhouse, a new building was constructed on a plot of land down the road.

The second Zacata Schoolhouse was apparently located at 2638 Zacata Road. A few of the remaining persons who attended the school still remember tales of how the children walked down the hilly incline to obtain water. When the school burned down, the children returned to the small, original schoolhouse on George Reed's property until the men of the community were able to build the third Zacata School.

On land across the road from Siloam Baptist Church was the site of the third Zacata Schoolhouse. Full of pride for their children's education, the community constructed the third schoolhouse using State of Virginia stock blueprints for a two-room schoolhouse and WPA funds in the 1930s. In the 1930s and 1940s, the number of children in Zacata continued to increase at such a rate that it was necessary to build an additional building. The larger building was used to educate the younger children.

The fourth Zacata School was built in the 1940s to accommodate the ever-increasing Zacata school population. Again, the community used stock school plans that were available from the State Department of Education for a two-room schoolhouse.

These past Zacata schoolteachers are listed, from left to right, as follows: Mrs. V. Weldon, Mrs. Rogers, Mrs. B.C. Tate, Mrs. E.F. Tompkins, and Mrs. Emily Tate.

Pictured here are Zacata teenage students.

A wonderful example of a creative teacher in Westmoreland County's schools, Bernice C. Tate penned the following poem for her students entitled "Secrets for Zacata Girls."

Secrets for Zacata
(Elementary Girls)
Zacata Girls' Social Code, 1951
*****WARNING******

Little teenage girl
   With stardust in your eyes
Hoping every boy may be
   Your Dream-Prince in disguise.

Enjoy your little dreams of love
   But a word of warning lass,
Just keep those dreams like lovely ships
   that thrill us as they pass.

The Dream Prince that you paint today
   With sweet illusion's brushes
Tomorrow may not be your type,
   So don't be in a rush.

Reality for teenage girls
   Can break your hasty heart
And marriage is a tragic thing
   For too young kids to start.

Throughout the rest of this chapter are group photographs of students and teachers at Zacata. (Courtesy of of Lloyd Willis, Sherman Tate, and Calvin Jenkins.)

This is another group photograph of a class of Zacata students.

These former Zacata students are revisiting their old school, which closed in 1958.

This former Zacata teacher is Mrs. Viola Weldon.

This former Zacata teacher is Mrs. Mazie Rogers.

This is a photograph of former Zacata teacher Mrs. Majorie Savage.

In this photograph, Miss Hall and Mrs. Ardell Hoban pose on the Zacata school steps.

Both these images capture two different classes at the Zacata School.

45

This picture captures the pride and excitement of these young Zacata students on the first day of school.

These three female students pose in front of the Zacata building.

Both of these photographs show two classes at the Zacata School.

Again, these photographs show two classrooms of Zacata students.

Sadie Roane was an industrial arts teacher who traveled throughout Westmoreland County giving students skills they would use for the rest of their lives.

Martha Lowe Jenkins Roane not only attended Zion School in Westmoreland County Schools, but came back to teach for 40 years. She was an active and devoted member of the community.

Templemans, a two-room Rosenwald school with an industrial arts room, was built in 1925

close to the site of a previous one-room schoolhouse.

This is a picture of the Templemans class of 1939.

53

In the early 1900s, the first Galilee School was a wood-framed building that lacked any type of indoor plumbing. Former students such as Joe Nelson recall how it was a quarter to half a mile to the Fones well to obtain water. Joseph Nelson attended this one-room schoolhouse in 1916 at the age of four instead of the normal age of seven and he attended the school until 1920 or 1921. He specifically recalled two of his teachers at Galilee, Jim Laws and Leverna Roane. Nelson, who graduated with a fourth-grade education, left Westmoreland County to serve during World War II; he can still quote the number of weeks, days, and hours he was away from his beloved county. Since that time, he has farmed and driven tractor trailers, but has never left Westmoreland County again.

The second Galilee School, seen here, was located in the Odd Fellows Hall, a short distance from a church. School board minutes reflect that this facility like many others lacked a well. In 1937, the Galilee School League partitioned the county school board for a well. The school eventually closed when the new Templemans School opened.

Varnelle Robinson Roane Ruffin was a native of Richmond. Mr. A.T. Johnson met her train in Fredericksburg and transported her to Westmoreland County. She taught for 43 years in Westmoreland County schools at Templemans, Potomac, and Cople-Montross.

Sebbie Jenkins attended Templemans School from primary to seventh grade as a child and returned to teach in 1945, upon graduating from Virginia State College, now Virginia State University.

Edna Jenkins Jones still recites poems learned in her youth for both young and old alike.

Three
COPLE SCHOOL DISTRICT

The first Zion School was built by the people of the church community on the ground where the Zion Church is now located. The school was situated to the left of the present-day church building. The school taught grades from primer to the seventh, according to Martha Lowe Jenkins Roane.

Armistead Tasker Johnson was the first teacher for the Zion School, and Ms. Betty L. Johnson was the second teacher at Zion.

This is a drawing of a Rosenwald school in the Cople District area. Early school district records show that the school board had only intended the second Zion School be constructed from plans for a one-room schoolhouse. However, since Rosenwald Funds were obtained, the school had to be built to the Rosenwald Committee's specifications. (Courtesy of Evelyn Jones.)

The Zion School opened on August 17, 1927, and did not close until the Cople District schools consolidated in 1958.

Housing grades one through seven, the Zion School had two large classrooms with a partition, two closets, and an industrial arts room, to which a Jeanes supervisor came each Thursday to teach arts and crafts to those who could afford to pay for the materials.

An interior view shows the teacher's platform in the front of the room.

The following students are pictured here: Jean Fulcher, Lottie Mae Ball, Alice Lee, Calvin Lee, Esther Mae Gaskins, Elizabeth Hall, Pearl Lee, Marie Johnson, Esther Gaskins, Robert Wilson, Gladys Hall, Barbara Burrell, Joyce Taylor, Bettie Lue Thompson, Ella Mae Thompson, Elizabeth Wilson, Helen Burrell, Walter "Billy" Turner, Carter Burrell, John Gaskins, Samuel "Webster" Newman, Bernard Newman, Richard Lee, William "Sonny" Clayton, Lewis Braxton, Lewis Carter Thompson, Walter Lee, Waverly Taylor, Charlie M. Wilson, James Phillip Hall, Ralph Wilson, Freddie Newman, Joe Newman, and Charles Taylor.

The following Zion School students appear, from left to right, as follows: (first row) Marie Johnson, Helen Burrell, and Esther Gaskins; (second row) Joyce Taylor, Peggy Clayton, Rose E. Wilson, Lue E. Johnson, Hattie Mae Fulcher, and Dorothy Ball; (third row) Yosif Roane, Lewis Braxton, Freddie Newman, Walter Lee, Thomas Wilson, Waverly Taylor, David Wilson, James Phillip Hall, Charles M. Wilson, and Carter Burrell (with face covered).

These Zion School students are, from left to right, as follows: (seated, on ground) Ella Mae Thompson, Alice Lee, and Clorice Burrell; (seated, chairs) William Lowe, Bettie Lue Thompson, Marie Conley, Esther Mae Gaskins, Virgie Smith, Calvin Lee, and Charles Taylors; (standing) John Gaskins, Elizabeth Hall, William Turner, Lottie Mae Ball, Gladys Hall, and Barbara Burrell.

This is a portrait of William "Sonny" Clayton.

As can be seen in this image, both older and younger students attended class together. These students include the following: Calvin Lee, Robert Wilson, Jean Fulcher, Denette Hughes, Marie Conley, Ella Mae Thompson, Esther Mae Gaskins, Bettie Lou Thompson, Clorice Burrell, Dorothy Johnson, Barbara Burrell, Earnell Fulcher, Mary Jones, Virgie Smith, Joe Newman, Charlie M. Wilson, Lottie Mae Ball, Joyce Taylor, William "Billy" Turner, Samuel "Webster" Newman, Gladys Hall, Peggy Clayton, Hattie Mae Fulcher, Elizabeth Wilson, Bertha Johnson, Scott Rich, Charles Taylor, Helen Burrell, Dorothy Ball, Marie Johnson, Lou E. Johnson, Rose E. Wilson, Lewis Braxton, William Lowe, Bernard Newman, William "Sonny" Clayton, Richard Lee, William Braxton, Clarence Rich, Carter Burrell, James Phillip Hall, Waverly Taylor, David Wilson, Lewis Thompson, Freddie Newman, and John Gaskins.

Walter Lee proudly poses for this school portrait.

As young Waverly Taylor would learn, books are an important part of the learning process.

Reverend Leon Baylor was a teacher at Zion School.

Sisters and former Zion students Lois Newman Ball and Alberta Newman Randall have learned to appreciate how important African-American history was and is in Westmoreland County. (Courtesy of Edward Hall.)

This is the site of the Odd Fellows Hall, now the property of Mrs. Ester Lee. When extra classroom space was needed, the children walked down the road to the Odd Fellows Hall.

Pictured here in 1948 on the first day of school are grandparents Hanna and John Green, who raised their grandchildren Geraldine Newman and Juanita Green.

Only left in the hearts and minds of the relatives are the tales of those who attended this simple one-room schoolhouse in the early 1900s. Not a trace remains on this field where corn and soy beans are planted today. Their were 22 Gordon children who lived nearby and attended its classroom. A very kind white teacher is said to have taught here when the school was in operation.

Rose Faunteroy Gordon was the parent of 22 children, all of whom attended Bethsaida School.

With only a little formal education, John Gordon made sure that his 22 children went to school.

The Gordon children are seen here and are listed as the following: Helen, Naomi, Bessie, Fannie, Margret, Rosie, Pearl, and Ruth, all of whom lived near the Bethsaida School.

Merril Gordon attended Bethsaida School and went on to serve his country.

Simmuel Gordon also proudly served his country.

72

The second Erica Schoolhouse was often referred to in late-1800s documents as the "Colored school near 'Black Ground'" because the soil in this area of Westmoreland County was very dark and rich. The second Erica School building was on what is now Erica Road. The ground for this school building was purchased in 1915 at a cost of $5 for 1 acre of land. The school league started on December 13, 1922, trying to get the Westmoreland County school board to erect a new school on the ground they had purchased, but the decision was postponed another year. The two-room building, with an industrial arts room /kitchen building, was finally erected. Rosenwald Funds were secured to keep the school open one month longer when county funds ran short for the black schools in 1930. In 1952, the schoolhouse had the same two-seater desks that had been there in the 1930s. This building was used as a schoolhouse until 1958, when it closed.

Austin Henry Ashton purchased the land for the Erica Schoolhouse. (Courtesy of Melanie Hall.)

In this 1938 Erica School class picture, these students are shown with their teachers, Reverend Albert Norman Johnson, who taught the upper grades, and his wife, Janie Johnson, who taught the lower grades. The children are as follows: (first row) Ben Cupid, Moses Johnson, Irvin Johnson, Walter Lane, James Newton, William Roane, Dick Johnson, Jimmy Smith, and James Wright; (second row) Gladys Lane, Margaret Lane, Ruth Johnson, Elma Ashton, Naomi Johnson, Ruth Lane, Rosie Tate, and Joseph A.T. Thompson. (between second and third rows) Robert Alma Johnson, Louise Smith, Bernice Lane, Carrie Thompson, Louise Thompson, Edna Thompson, Pearl Lane, and Edna Newton; (third row) Ed Smith, Robert Crabbe, Robert Hackett, Martha Thompson, Coretta Cupid, Rachel Wright, Elizabeth Hill, Lucy Butler, Rose Cupid, Leon Tate, Robert Thompson, and Howard Thompson; (row fourth) Annie Mae Roane, Lucy Hackett, and teachers Reverend Johnson, Mrs. Johnson, Lucy Wright, and Gertrude Johnson.

Melanie Hall is seen here standing on the site of the two-room schoolhouse that closed in 1958.

As can be seen here, May Day in 1948 was a time of great fun for students.

Captain Billy Smith, a young 94-year-old gentleman, recalls the first Frog Hall School being across the dirt road from where the new school was being built. Taught by Miss Clara Seldon in a building that had once been a store owned by a black family, the schoolhouse was referred to as the "Club Store" by many of the students.

A larger schoolhouse was needed to educate the large number of youths in the Frog Hall area. Funding for the new school came from the Frog Hall Colored School League, the Westmoreland County School Board, and the Rosenwald Fund. The new, more modern school opened in November of 1928 across the rural dirt road from the first schoolhouse. Some

Frog Hall Colored School
Westmoreland Co., Va.
Nov. 1928.

remember going over to the old building at recess to run around and play. The schoolhouse name was changed about 1937 to Sandy Point School. Many times when the post office of an area changed its name so did the school. Mail was especially important to teachers, who had left family elsewhere to teach in Westmoreland County. (Photo courtesy of Library of Virginia.)

Sara Smith Wilson at age 97 is the older sister of Captain Billy, but she was so small she could not make the long walk to school until she was nine or ten years old. She attended school until she was 17 and had completed the seventh grade. Desks were used only by the children in the higher grades, and younger students put their books in their laps and sat on benches placed throughout the room. During recess, she enjoyed sewing on a piece of fabric, and her hands are still busy today.

Annie Courtney Smith attended the first Frog Hall school.

Because such a larger number of children attended the school, a small-frame chapel at the corner of Sandy Point Road and Tucker Hill Road was used as an auxiliary classroom.

William Walter Wilson, referred to by many simply as Uncle Jim, was a much respected teacher in Westmoreland County.

Frog Hall teacher Laura Courtney Conley was the first black schoolteacher in Westmoreland County.

Lillian Dowling is a well-remembered Sandy Point teacher.

Edna Hazel Newton Smith Crabbe, a native Westmorelander, attended the Erica Elementary School and A.T. Johnson High School. Upon completion of college, she returned to teach for many years at Sandy Point, until the school closed in 1958.

Sandy Point students included this father-daughter pair, Leslie Wilson and Joyce Wilson Jones, who can still recall fond memories of their elementary schoolhouse.

Teacher Melinda Russ Selden taught her class at Frog Hall to make taffy on the wood stove.

The Westmoreland County School Board had given $700 for this wood-framed two-room schoolhouse, the second Hacketts Hill School, but by March 13, 1929, the school league committee came back to the school board requesting that an acre of land be purchased from L.W. English to be added to the present school site. Used as a schoolhouse until 1958, this structure is used today as the fellowship hall for New Jerusalem Baptist Church.

Brother Sherman Jackson and sister Adele Page Roane never did complain about school because it was an honor to be allowed to attend. As children, they walked up to 7 miles one way to school; they even used a small boat to cut across the creeks to save themselves from walking so far.

Annie Brown taught at Hacketts Hill School from 1924 to 1926.

Hackett Hill students Bessie Green and Mary Ester Gaskins are seen here in this 1930s image.

85

Nena Fisher Crabbe was a student at Hacketts Hill school in the 1920s.

Kremlin School was remolded and is used today as a community center by the Jerusalem Baptist Church.

The Kremlin School started as one of five private schools in Westmoreland County. Taught by Mrs. Judith McCoy Johnson, classes were held in a building called Hall's Store. The first public Kremlin School, probably a one-room log house, was opened in 1870. The second Kremlin School, seen here, was a Rosenwald School building; its cornerstone carries that date of July 4, 1919. Among those who taught here were Jones Atwell, Ms. Pollard, Ms. Elaine Johnson, Mrs. Velma Rodgers Morris, and Ms. Philippa Stowe.

This 1930s image shows a group of Kremlin schoolchildren.

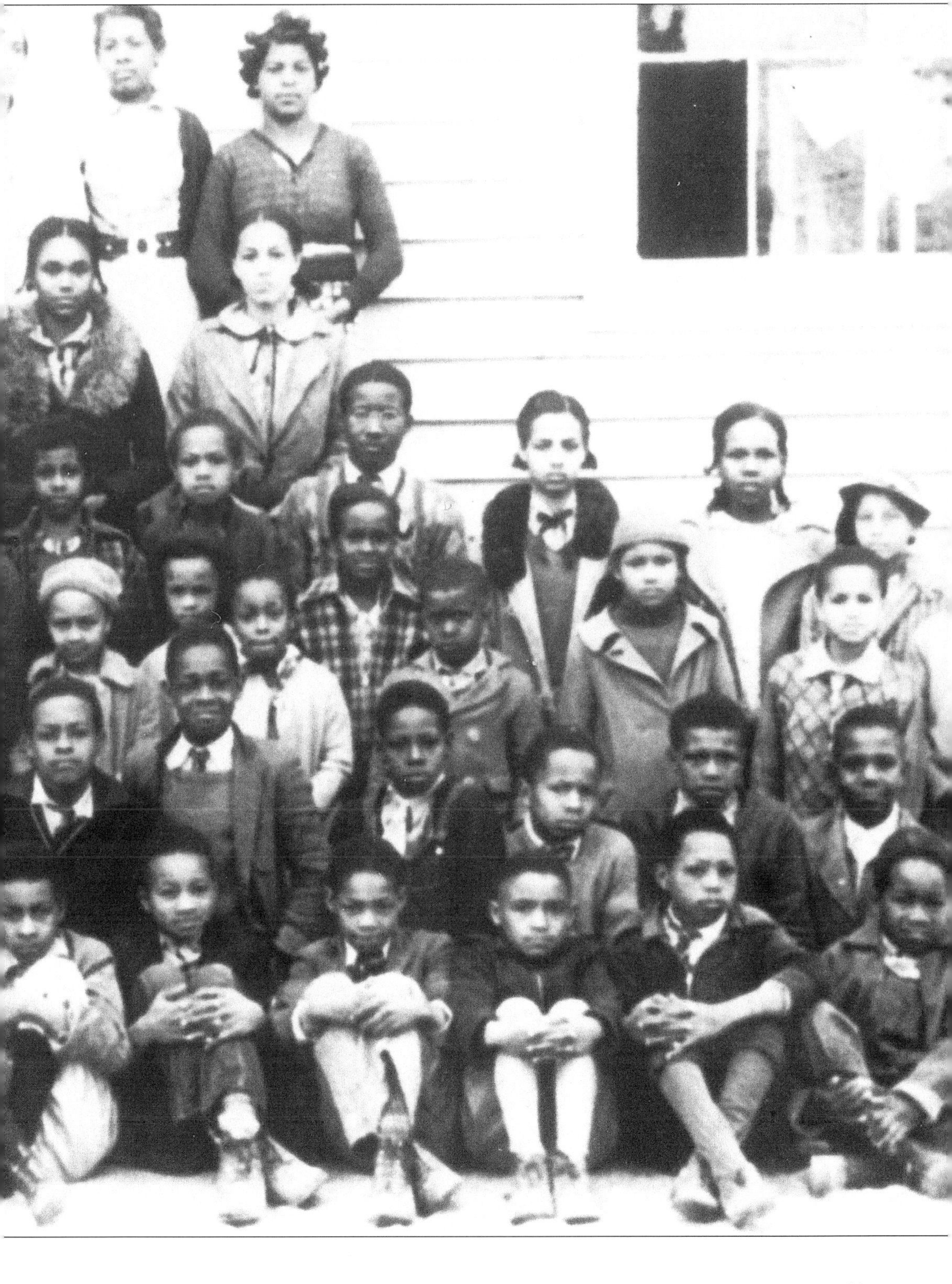

Teacher Velma Rodgers Morris taught at the Kremlin school from 1926 to 1930.

This is a rare image of the Mudbridge School.

The first Mudbridge school was in operation during the late 1800s. According to Tom Smith, this one-room schoolhouse had a hallway as you entered to hang your coats. The school housed grades up to the seventh. If a student was really smart, he or she might have the opportunity to repeat the seventh grade, for many times, the families did not have enough money to send him or her away to high school. Teachers at this school included Ms. Mary Edwards and Ms. Mattie Faunteroy from Pennsylvania. The school burned down about 1921 and the children went to class in a chapel. Tuesday was devoted to Industrial Arts Day, in which the boys learned to make ax handles using a broken piece of glass and clothes pins; the girls learned to sew and can. The boys who went here were referred to as the "Mudbridge Boys." Of course, the area was known for its "mud."

These Mudbridge children, Carrol Smith, Annie Smith, Buluah Smith Lewis, and Henry Smith, can sing the famous Mudbridge song.

Dating back to the late 1800s, the first Potomac School was a one-room log cabin. Rebuilt after a fire as a wooden frame structure, the Potomac School had two rooms; then after another fire and another reconstruction, it became a three-room schoolhouse. As a three-room schoolhouse, the Potomac School had the distinction of being the first black school in Westmoreland County to offer a public high school education, from 1931 to 1937. The Potomac School closed in 1958, when the Cople District Schools consolidated. Some of the teachers that taught at the Potomac School include Ms. Lillian Dowling and Ms. Bertha Baily Burnett.

This is Potomac teacher Lara Brown.

The deed to the land in which Salem School was located upon was dated 1885. Exactly when a wooden frame schoolhouse was built is unknown. Salem School, by newspaper accounts, is known to have been there in the late 1800s across the road from the Salem Church, on what is now Erica Road. Except for the small addition on the side, the one-room schoolhouse, which closed in 1958, was little changed from when it was first built. Teachers included Lulu Landon Smith, Mary Thompson Smith, Mr. Marie Johnson, and Reverend Baylor.

Teacher Mary Thompson Smith, from Pennsylvania, taught at Salem for many years.

Four
ROSENWALD SCHOOLS

Program Rosenwald School Day
FRIDAY, MARCH 3, 1933

1. SONG—America.
2. PRAYER—By local minister or church officer.
3. Statement giving (1) the purpose of the meeting, (2) the benefit of a good school to the community, (3) the general condition of the school, and (4) the outstanding needs of the school—by the principal or one of the teachers.
4. Sixteen important facts about Negro schools in Virginia—By sixteen pupils of the school, each pupil giving one fact.
5. SPECIAL MUSIC—By the school.
6. ADDRESS—Hon. Julius Rosenwald and what he has done to advance Negro education in the South—By teacher.
7. SONG—Negro National Anthem, or some other suitable selection.
8. ADDRESS—What the people of the community should do for their school—By local minister or interested citizen.
9. COLLECTION—Money to be kept for school improvements.
10. SONG—By the assembly.
11. ADJOURNMENT.

This outlines the different events for a program held on March 3, 1933, for the Rosenwald School. (Courtesy Virginia State Department of Education.)

A Brief History of Julius Rosenwald and His Philanthropy

An American of Jewish German heritage, Julius Rosenwald was born on August 12, 1862, in Springfield, Illinois, not far from the birthplace of Abraham Lincoln. As a boy, he attended the historic occasion of the dedication of a monument to Lincoln in 1874 and shook hands with President Ulysses S. Grant. His early work would be as a tailor; thus, he started a company that made men's suits. One of Rosenwald's "best" customers would be Richard Sears, and Rosenwald was impressed by Sears's ability to sell large quantities of men's suits. Mr. Sears of Sears and Roebucks was a very pleased customer.

While Rosenwald was described as an unaggressive salesman, he did capture Mr. Sears's interest and sold his ideas to him. Sears, although one of history's greatest salesman, had a hard time delivering to customers what they had ordered. It would take Rosenwald, who came to work for him, to introduce improvements that allowed orders to be processed more efficiently, which increased sales an incredible 500%. Between 1901 and 1905, by issuing money-back guarantees and insisting on honest merchandise for less money, Rosenwald believed people would buy more. By treating people fairly, honestly, and generously, Rosenwald believed that the customers' response back would be fair, honest, and generous.

In 1906 Rosenwald convinced Sears and Roebuck to build a 40-acre warehouse and to create a schedule system that allowed employees to handle 100,000 orders per day; so impressive was this system that Henry Ford modified it for Ford Motors.

On November 21, 1908, Rosenwald became chairman of the board of Sears and Roebucks. As he traveled throughout the South on behalf of Sears and Roebuck, Rosenwald, like President Lincoln, noticed the plight of the blacks. Rosenwald became interested in helping the black community in 1911 after reading Booker T. Washington's autobiography *Up from Slavery*. According to Rosenwald biographer M.R. Werner, he was struck by this particular passage: "My experience is that there is something in human nature which always makes an individual recognize and reward merit, no matter under what colour of skin merit is found, I have found too, that it is the visible, the tangible, that goes along way in softening prejudices, the actual sight of a first class house that a Negro has built is ten times more potent than pages of discussion about a house that he ought to build, or perhaps could build."

In 1917, he established for the "Well being of Mankind" the Julius Rosenwald Fund. The fund had two objectives: 1. to bring decent education to Negro children in the South; 2. alleviate Jewish distress in the Middle East. Designed not to be a perpetual endowment, Rosenwald's Fund was set up as follows: "Permanent endowments tends to lessen the amount available for immediate needs, and our immediate needs are too plain and too urgent to allow us to do the work of future generations." He instructed his trustees to spend itself out of existence within 25 years of his death—they did so in 15 years.

Rosenwald's philanthropy, particularly toward African Americans, was to promote self reliance and self help. He believed success was 95% luck and 5% ability. His school building plan sought to help people who wanted to help themselves. By the time he died in 1932, Rosenwald had contributed $4 million to help build 5,357 schools in the South. This was matched by $18.1 million in government funds, $1.2 million from other foundations, and $4.7 million from African Americans. The latter funds were the most important because no school was built unless blacks were willing to contribute funds. When asked what endeavor gave him greatest satisfaction, Rosenwald replied "The work with the colored people." Rosenwald was a quiet family man who loved to play tennis at his home, called Ravinia, outside of Chicago until a heart condition forced him to take up golf.

As can be seen in this inside view of the school, small hooks were used to hang the children's coats.

Rosenwald schools had good construction specifications that had to be met.

Student Starnsha Henry exams the solid construction of this existing building.

The Rosenwald School was the second Chandler Mill Pond schoolhouse for the African-

American children. A two-room schoolhouse was built in 1922.

STATE DEPARTMENT OF EDUCATION OF VIRGINIA

RICHMOND, VA., *February 8, 1933.*

To the Colored Teachers of Virginia.

DEAR TEACHER:

Rosenwald Day this year should receive special attention inasmuch as our great benefactor has recently passed away. We are asking that all colored schools in our State observe March 3rd as Rosenwald Day—a day which is being observed over the whole South.

Please get permission from your division superintendent to use the afternoon session of March 3rd as a time for honoring Mr. Julius Rosenwald. It is desired that you will invite all your children, your patrons and friends to your school for these afternoon exercises and do honor to the man who has been so helpful to the cause of Negro education all over the Southland.

Please keep in mind the following suggestions with reference to the purpose of this occasion and the arrangement of your program:

1. To bring all the people together at the schoolhouse on the afternoon of March 3rd for the purpose of getting better acquainted with one another and with the school and its needs.

2. To show what progress, if any, the school and community have made within the past ten years.

3. To study the needs of the school and to meet these needs by raising the necessary funds.

4. To show the appreciation of the people for all past favors rendered by the public school authorities of the county and by other agencies such as the Rosenwald Fund, the Jeanes and Slater Funds and the General Education Board, which have rendered material and timely assistance in the stimulation and development of Negro schools in Virginia.

5. To rededicate ourselves to the cause of education of all the children of our beloved Commonwealth.

It is hoped that the principal or one of the teachers will develop these statements and in a fitting and forceful speech of about ten minutes acquaint the audience with the purpose of the meeting.

This is a message from the Virginia's State Department of Education regarding Rosenwald Day and its observance across the South.

ROSENWALD SCHOOL SPECIFICATIONS

In the Rosenwald School Specifications, the Fund stated the following: "there should be racial cooperation between the races requiring local contributions from Blacks and Whites . . . local school system had to contribute to construction and agree to maintain the building as part of their school system."

As for the architectural designs for the schools, the Fund gave these specifications: "each school to be of a white frame construction . . . emphasis given to proper light and ventilation both in paint colors and size of windows . . . advocated an Industrial Arts room . . . movable partitions often used to convert classrooms into a meeting room or an auditorium which could serve as a community center . . . schools had one to four classrooms . . . desired school be on 2 acres of land in rural areas and to have a garden. The Fund assembled standard plans for various types of buildings which were used by all schools receiving aid and were made available to school authorities generally.

Repair and Improvement of School Buildings and Grounds

Every schoolteacher should carefully check the following items as they exist in the school where she is teaching, and where improvements can be made with little outlay of capital by enlisting free labor and materials from the community, such improvements and repairs should be made as may be necessary to the safety of the building and the occupants. There are many little items of repair and improvements that will go a long way toward arousing and stimulating interest on the part of the patrons of the community, which call for little outlay of capital if the teacher is willing to take the initiative in arousing a community's interest. In many buildings there are conditions about the building that contribute to insanitary conditions, and contribute to actual danger to the building, due to unsafe chimneys, stoves, electric-wiring, steps needing repair, broken window glass, permitting draughts directly on pupils, doors without locks, thus inviting a tramp to occupy the building overnight or during shut-down periods, etc., all of which can be corrected with little outlay of capital, provided the community or different members of the community are willing to donate some labor.

The following list of items should be carefully checked by a the teacher, and where there is an opportunity the teacher should interest the patrons of the community in assisting in making the corrections.

Outside Paint: This includes painting the main school building as well as the privies and other outhouses.

Repairing Woodwork: This includes such items as broken siding, broken window frames and sash, unsafe steps, porch floors, etc.

Repairing Roofs and Downspouts: Leaking roofs, rusted, worn-out, and broken gutters and downspouts.

Chimneys: The stove pipe should not be closer than 3 inches to wall at any point, and should be well supported throughout. Where the stove pipe enters the chimney the joints should be tight. Rusted and worn-out stove pipes should be replaced.

Inside Painting: Walls to classrooms should be painted light color. A cold water paint is good if better cannot be secured. The ceiling should be ivory, cream, or light buff. The wainscotting should be dark buff or tan.

Window Shades: Should operate and should be a light buff color.

Plaster: Plaster repairs can easily be made by using patching plaster.

Outhouses: Privies should in all cases be made sanitary and fireproof. Frequently by digging a new pit, moving the privy to a new location close to the old location, covering up the old pit with dirt . . . from the new pit, repairing the seats and providing lids that will stay closed when not in use, making the building water-tight, and so closing up the seats and the building under seats that flies cannot get into the excreta, will accomplish much by the way of improving health conditions in the community. Bulletins may be secured from the State Board of Health on the proper treatment of the pit privy.

School Grounds: By planting small trees from the woods, such as pine and cedar, and by planting laurel and other shrubbery native to the community, school grounds can be greatly improved at practically no cost, except labor for doing the necessary grading. Grass seed can be sown at no cost except for the seed, provided the labor is furnished. Precaution should be taken in sowing grass or planting shrubs to see that they are so planted that tall grass cannot grow close to the school building, and in dry summer months set fire to the building in the event a fire is started in the tall dry grass.

Blackboards: Defective blackboards can be repaired by applying an inexpensive blackboard paint in accordance with manufacturer's directions.

Teachers are urged to give due consideration to all minor repairs that may be necessary to make the building safe, comfortable and sanitary. Where special problems come up that seriously affect the safety of the building, the teacher should communicate with the division superintendent, advising him of such problems needing attention and correction.

This is a present-day view of the inside of a Rosenwald schoolhouse.

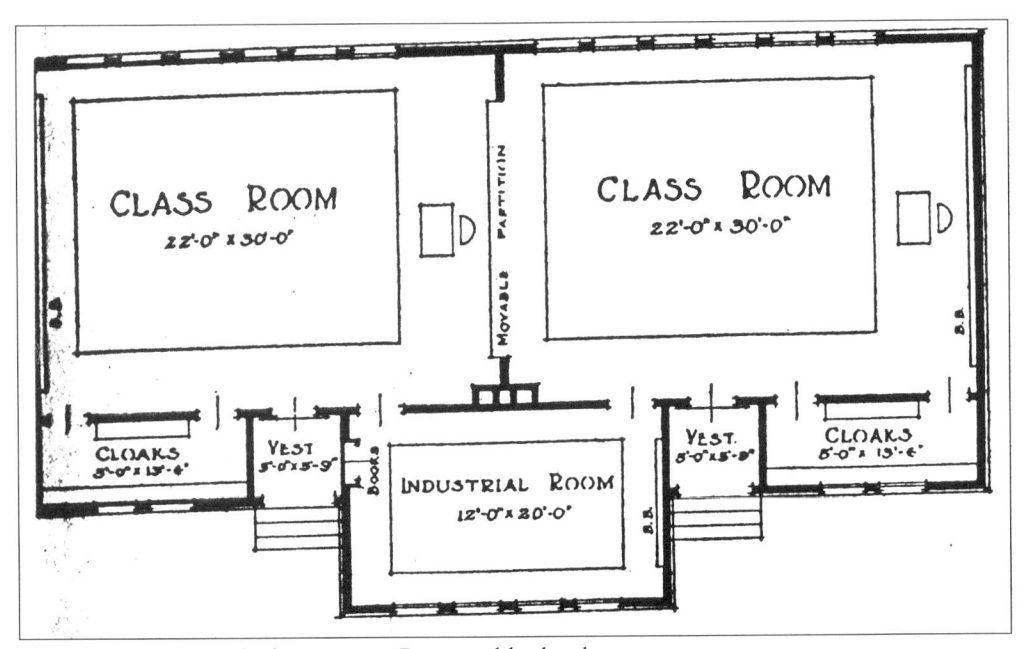

These are floorplans for laying out a Rosenwald school.

This letter from the superintendent of public instruction informs readers about the observance of Rosenwald Day. (Courtesy of State Department of Education Records.)

COMMONWEALTH OF VIRGINIA

STATE BOARD OF EDUCATION

RICHMOND, VA., *February* 8, 1933.

For the past several years it has been the custom of the State Department of Education to issue a bulletin carrying suggestions with reference to the observance of Rosenwald Day. The observance of the day this year presents a significant opportunity to pay real tribute to Mr. Julius Rosenwald, who has been such a friend to the development of Negro education in the South.

The late Mr. Rosenwald was undoubtedly one of the greatest friends that the South has ever had in the development of public education for the Negroes. Nothing that the Negro race can do by way of commemorating his life and by way of paying allegiance to him and his work, is capable of indicating the deep gratitude that should be held towards him. No program or exercise can by any means indicate the real love and esteem that was held for him. Nevertheless, every effort should be made this year to observe Rosenwald Day in a way that will indicate to the fullest possible extent the abiding faith and respect that was had for him. In setting aside in the Negro schools a day to be known as Rosenwald Day, I am fully cognizant of the fact that this year, as never before, the Negroes of the South should pay distinct homage to Mr. Rosenwald and what he has done for them.

SIDNEY B. HALL,
Superintendent of Public Instruction.

THINGS TO BE DONE BY THE PRINCIPAL AND TEACHERS

1. Strive to get all the colored people in your community to the meeting on Friday, March 3rd.
2. Work out all the details and make the program successful.
3. There are sixteen statements which should be assigned to sixteen different students who can commit the statements to memory and present them forcefully to the audience.
4. A few facts about Mr. Rosenwald are given which should be used in the development of the address by a teacher.
5. We are enclosing a blank which is to be used by the principal in making a report of the condition of the school, the success of the meeting, and the amount collected for the school. This report is to be returned to the State Agent for Negro Schools as soon as convenient after the meeting, but no money should be sent.
Wishing each of you great success, I am

This note details what needs to be done by principals and teachers for the upcoming Rosenwald Day. (Courtesy of Virginia State Superintendent Association.)

Sixteen Important Facts about Black Education in Virginia

1. In 1917, the cost of instruction per child was $2.58, while for the session of 1930–31, the cost was above $14, an increase of more than $11 per child.

2. The total number of black children enrolled in schools in 1917 was 132,316. In 1930–31, the total number of children enrolled was 158,914.

3. In 1917, the average attendance of black children was 90,039, while in 1930 the average attendance was nearly 125,000.

4. Great improvements have been made at the State College at Petersburg, within the last few years. Four or five new dormitories have been erected. At the present time, a new dining hall is being built at the school.

5. In addition to the State College at Petersburg, other schools that are doing teacher training in Virginia are Hampton Institute, Virginia Union University, and St. Paul's (Methodist Episcopal) College.

6. In 1917, there were 2,495 teachers employed in the black schools in the state, while in 1930–31, there were nearly 4,000 teachers—a large increase.

7. In 1917, the average annual salary of black teachers was $170.06. In 1930–31, the average salary of an elementary teacher alone was in excess of $500.

8. The average length of a session was 127 days in 1917, and this increased to 164 days in 1930.

9. In 1917 there were only six county training schools in the state. In 1930–31, there were 54 county training schools, 10 of which were placed on the accreditation list.

10. In 1917, a total of 56 Jeanes agents, working in 50 different counties, raised about $46,000 for various school enterprises, while in 1930–31, 60 such teachers raised approximately $100,000 for the same purposes.

11. In 1917, there were only a few Rosenwald buildings in Virginia. In 1930–31, there were approximately 400.

12. The Slater Board gave $12,500 toward helping the 50 county training schools during 1930–31.

13. The Jeanes Board gave $12,500 toward helping to pay salaries of 60 Jeanes agents last session, with the balance coming from the state and counties.

14. For 1930–31, the federal government gave $17,000 for Vocational Agriculture and Home Economics through the Smith-Hughes Fund.

15. In 1930–31, the total amount of $22,400.33 was spent for Negro Trade and Industrial classes throughout the state. Of this amount the federal government gave $4,556.77, while a similar amount was paid by the state. The balance came from local funds.

16. The 5,000 Rosenwald school was the Greenbrier School, a six-teacher brick building in Elizabeth City near Hampton.

This is an image of a seventh grade class. In June 1958, the last of the the Cople and Montross District's one- and two-room black schoolhouses closed their doors. The September of that same year saw children bused from their neighborhood schools to a larger facility with individual classrooms for each grade and a separate teacher for each classroom. Though the Cople-Montross School was built without a cafeteria, it did have a central heating system so that the teacher no longer had to worry with a wood stove for heat. There were large windows for light and ventilation, and the teachers and students were overjoyed with their new school.

The following are Washington District teachers: Mrs. Ethel Lomax, Mrs. Dorothy Payne, Mrs. Ardel Hoban, and Principal Walker.

105

This is a picture of the first faculty at Cople-Montross Elementary. They are, from left to right as follows: (seated) Lola Graham (Hacketts Hill); Myrtle Smith (Erica); Laura Brown (Potomac); Mary T. Smith (Salem); Bernice Tate (Zacata); Olie O. Smith (principal); Viola W. Maiden (Hacketts Hill); Vernell R. Ruffin (Templemans); Lureatha J. Harris (Zion); and Elsie Johnson (secretary); (standing, front row) Waverly Taylor Jr.; Lucille Jackson; Mazie Rogers (Erica); Edna S. Crabbe (Sandy Point); Mattie P. Lowe (Potomac); Sallie B. Lee (Kremlin); Frances Jenkins (Mudbridge); Bertha Burnett (Potomac); Martha J. Roane (Templemans); Bettie L. Johnson (Zion); Lenora Bagvy (Salem); Queenie Ford (Zion); Emily Crabbe; Theadora Weldon (Kremlin); Dallas Branson; and Yosif Roane; (standing, back row) Emily Tate (Zacata); Lillian L. Dowling (Sandy Point); and Viola W. Jones (Zacata).

Lillian Dowling was a former Sandy Point teacher and is seen here hard at work at Cople-Montross Elementary School. Cople-Montross Elementary and Washington District Elementary provided better educational facilities for the black students, although the district still segregated education.

Five
Typical School Days
Teachers and Lesson Plans

This is what Walter Miller's trunk would have looked like as he was sent away to school prior to 1930.

It took until 1905, a total of 35 years after the public education process began in Westmoreland County, Virginia, for citizens to begin thinking about a high school that would educate their children past the seventh grade. After local prejudices against public education had been broken down by persistent propaganda and financial aid, the General Education Board, or John D. Rockerfeller's fund, was able to help gradually establish educational facilities. Like many early education reforms, concentration first focused on improving the white schools so that there would be less resistance in communities when assistance was given to the black schools. In 1910 a white high school was open in each magisterial district of Colonial Beach, Oak Grove, Montross, Cople, and Kinsale.

Persons of color either ended their education or were sent away by boat to relatives or kind friends who would provide room and board so that children could be educated in Philadelphia, Baltimore, or Washington, D.C. A few private boarding high schools existed, but these institutions were expensive and only a few black children could attend.

When A.T. Johnson High School opened in 1937, it was a proud day in Westmoreland County black history. In 1998, A.T. Johnson High school was designated a National Historic Landmark.

A student of Sugarland School, Mrs. Hoban went on to become the first black woman to teach in an all-white school and was also the first black female principal in Westmoreland County.

Here are some of Westmoreland County's finest teachers relaxing outside of the classroom during a summer session at Virginia State.

WESTMORELAND COUNTY TEACHERS

In the Westmoreland County schools, teachers were respected, held in high esteem, and given a place of honor in the African-American community. These men and women were educators, social workers, dieticians, custodians, and persons of high moral character and integrity. These teachers showed a tremendous talent for creativity and the ability to teach well in a simple setting that did not allow easy access to books. When textbooks were scarce, these teachers used what they had and taught their students to memorize. Because of the close connection between the church and schools and the fact that they were often one in the same, the subject of religion played an integral role in the educational process, and many times, the Bible and Biblical stories were used to teach these students.

In 1887, Westmoreland County spent 85¢ to educate a child, and the county only had 38 schoolhouses: 21 white schools and 17 black schools. The county was split into three districts, Cople, Montross, and Washington.

Cople District	Montross District	Washington District
6 buildings	3 buildings	8 buildings
930 students	314 students	704 students
4 colored teachers	3 colored teachers	3 colored teachers

In 1893 the county's educational system increased and there were 42 schools in Westmoreland County: 23 frame buildings and 19 log buildings; 24 white schools and 18 black schools. All were one-room structures, only seven had desks, and none were graded schools. In the superintendent's report, he details that of the 42 teachers in the county, 35 were white and only 7 were "colored." The work they have done speaks well of them.

Cople District	Montross District	Washington District
7 buildings	3 buildings	8 buildings
1,013 students	289 students	780 students

By 1900, we had 46 school buildings: 41 were frame and 5 log. The county was proud to report that three schools had been built that year and eight outhouses. Thirty schools had good furniture and 13 had desks, and 35 buildings were now owned by the county. Thomas Brown, superintendent of schools, reported that he knew of no private schools supervised by the district. He reported that the seating capacity of the 27 white school buildings was 1,000, and the 19 "colored" school building had a seating capacity of 615.

Cople District	Montross District	Washington District	Colonial Beach
7 buildings	4 buildings	8 buildings	2 buildings
1,029 students	268 students	739 students	not reported
1 colored (c) teacher	3 teachers (c)	3 teachers (c)	2 teachers (c)

In 1921, the cost for educating a white child was $15 as opposed to $9 to educate a black child on the elementary level. While 113 white children went to county-supported high schools, black children did not have a school to obtain a high school education and thus, had to be sent away for that education. Looking at the salary structure, a white male teacher was paid $1,500, a white female, $480, while black teachers made $350 and $300, respectively. Each school district now had a school league. Black students were reported as "856 colored males and 926 colored females." There were 19 one-room and 4 two-room black schoolhouses.

Cople District	Montross District	Washington District	Colonial Beach
10 buildings	4 buildings	9 buildings	1 building

Susan H. Howard, born into slavery, remembered vividly how on the day the Civil War ended she had been made ready to be sold by her owners, and as news arrived that the war was over she was suddenly free. Her descendants include several fine Westmoreland County schoolteachers: Maude Ware, Pauline Washington, and Lucille Ware, her granddaughter and a historian.

This is an image of Mrs. Richards, who was active with the Eltham school league.

111

Yosif Roane, a Zion School student, is pictured with the flag, which was respected daily.

God and Country

God was always put first, for the school day started with a devotional reading from the Bible. Country was also remembered daily, as children proudly saluted the flag and pledged their allegiance to America. Songs both to God and Country were sung with real commitment. Lessons would be taught by age group because desks were not always available, so a group of children would sit together on a bench while being instructed on their lesson. Those students not being taught would do assigned work quietly so that the teacher could give full attention to the group he or she was instructing. Many times, one teacher often had 40 or more students. The teacher commanded full respect and had control of his/her classroom. Children were eager to learn and realized that education was a privilege. Teachers were extremely creative and did not let a shortage of textbooks or supplies hamper their teaching.

The schoolhouse fire was usually started by an older boy who arrived at school early. Lessons consisted of reading, writing, arithmetic, geography, and history; a ten-minute recess broke up the day in the morning and afternoon. On special days, an industrial arts teacher or a Jeanes supervisor would come to teach basic skills, such as sewing and cooking to the girls and woodshop to the boys.

Lunchtime was a part of the day spent playing and eating. The afternoon consisted of more learning. If all the lessons were finished by Friday afternoon, the children would then study their Sunday school lesson since the schoolteacher and sunday schoolteacher were often one in the same. At the end of the day, the schoolhouse floors were oiled down and the blackboard cleaned. Pride was taken to leave the classroom neat and clean.

SCHOOL LUNCH

A typical school lunch consisted of whatever Mother had on hand. Children were just happy to be going to school.

No lunch money was needed. No cafeteria was available. No choices were given. Early lunches were comprised of whatever Mama had on hand. Lunch, usually carried in a molasses tin bucket, consisted most often of a freshly made biscuit with preserves. The most common preserves were citron, red and green tomatoes, pear, fig, and strawberry that had been picked by the children and canned by Mama. A hard-boiled egg, a sweet potato, occasionally a piece of meat from breakfast, or a fatback was placed on the biscuit; however, some children, such as Joe Nelson, still remember being told the following: "If you want to be smart, you don't eat meat." Treats such as apples were stored in pine needles so that they would last as far into the winter as possible. Oranges provided by the government surplus food program, peanut butter, and cheese added variety to the children's diet. As a special treat, molasses or pulled taffy was made on the wood stove.

The only beverage was water, which had to be drawn from the well or neighboring stream or spring in a wooden bucket. Some schools had only one dipper, and all drank from the common dipper. Cod liver oil was dispensed daily, and again, like the dipper, there was only one spoon to use for all. In cold weather, caring teachers would place a big pot on the wood stove, and parents would send in home-canned vegetables for a nutritious hot vegetable soup. Many a sweet potato was sent to school and placed on the wood stove to provide a warm and nutritious meal.

Concerning lunch in the 1940s through 1958, Sebbie Jenkins remembers that for 3¢, a child could buy a hot government subsidized lunch, which the teacher often had to cook. Also, she recalls that there was more variety and that the meals were nutritious. Government surplus also provided for those unable to buy their lunch. White sandwich bread for lunches did not become common until the 1950s in the rural community of Westmoreland County.

School Board Minutes
November 14, 1934

"It was decided to purchase a lard tin and a five-gallon kettle for each of the Negro schools to be used in cooking and serving a hot lunch under the F.F.R.A."

In this image, Malachi Burton examines the old school water pump.

School Lunch Recipes for Treats

Molasses Taffy
- 1 cup granulated sugar
- 1 cup brown sugar
- 2 cups light molasses
- 3/4 cup water
- 1/4 cup butter
- 1/8 teaspoon baking soda
- 1/4 teaspoon salt

Directions:
1. Put the sugar, molasses, and water into a saucepan and cook until candy thermometer reaches 265 degrees. It is necessary to cook the candy slowly and stir it to prevent it from burning.
2. Remove saucepan from the fire and add butter, soda, and salt; stir until mixed well.
3. Turn the hot mixture onto a sheet pan spayed with Pam or covered in parchment paper. Allow to stand until cool enough to handle. It helps to butter the hands slightly.
4. Form a ball and pull until rather firm and of a light yellow color.
5. Stretch out in a long rope and cut into pieces (about 70 pieces 1 inch long).

School Lunch Recipes for Treats

Old Fashioned Pulled Candy
- 3 cups sugar
- 1 cup sorghum molasses
- 2 tablespoons vinegar
- 2 tablespoons butter

Directions:
1. Mix ingredients in an iron skillet and bring to a boil, stirring only until the sugar is dissolved.
2. When a little of the syrup reaches the hard crack stage, pour into a shallow buttered pan.
3. If desired, add peppermint flavoring or other flavorings and pieces of black walnuts.
4. When cool enough to handle, butter hands, pull until its hard to stretch, twist into long ropes, and cut with scissors into small pieces.

School Lunch Recipes for Treats

Citron Preserves
   1 citron
   2 cups of sugar for every cup of peeled citron

Directions:
1. In a large roasting pan, place a fresh citron that has been wiped off and bake in oven at 200 degrees for one hour, until a little soft.
2. Remove and allow to cool slightly, then peel. Flesh will still be firm, but it will be easy to cut the melon, remove the seeds, and save seeds to grow future watermelons. 3. Cut the yellow-looking flesh into small pieces so that about three pieces will fit on a biscuit.
4. Place the melon in a large pot and add 2 cups of sugar for each heaping cup of melon.
5. Let the sugar melon sit overnight.
6. The next morning, cook on top of the stove until the melon is tender and the mixture has thickened.
7. Cook until the syrup drips off the spoon and carefully place the hot contents in sterilized canning jars and then seal.

(Courtesy of Mama Nellie Gaskins.)

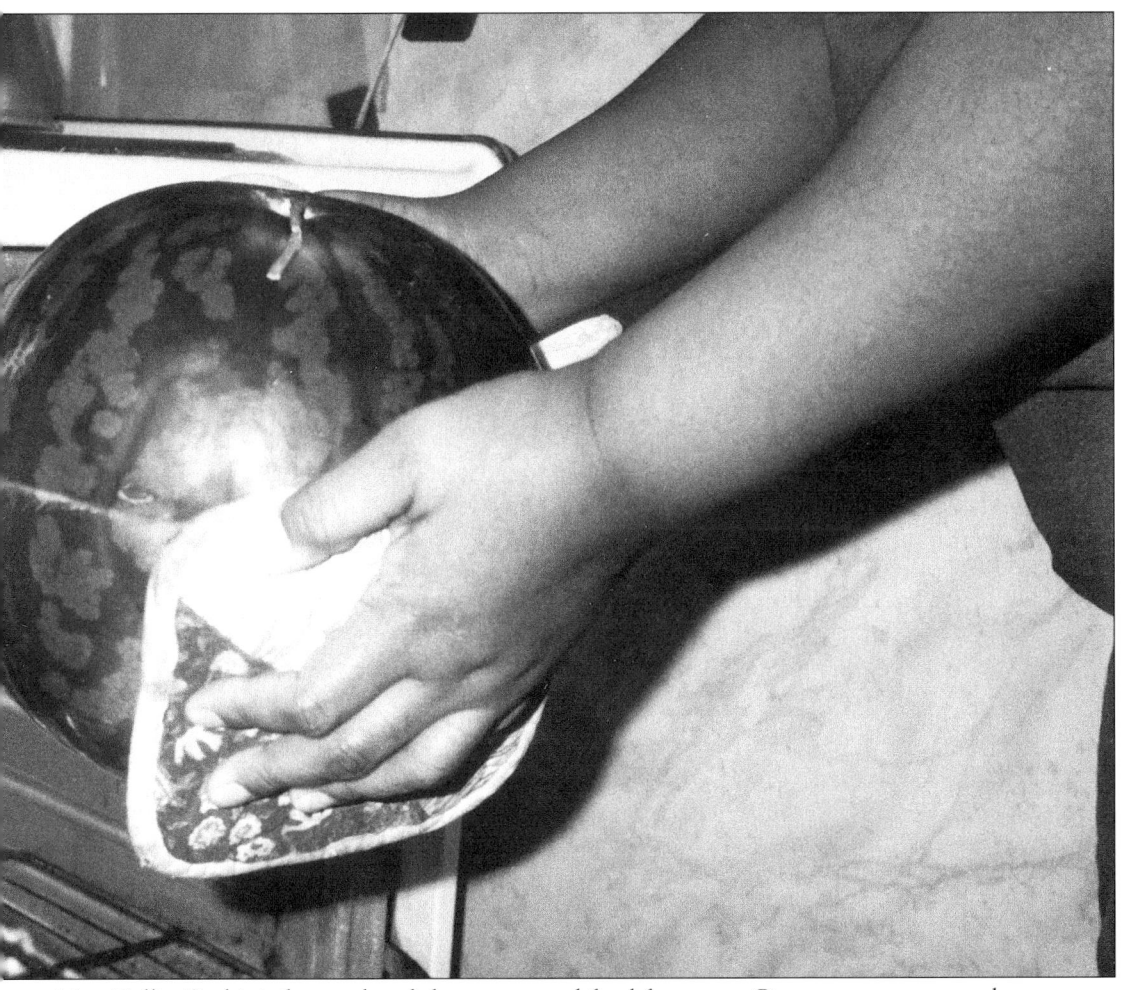

Mrs. Nellie Gaskin's famous hands have prepared food for many. Citron preserves served on a biscuit was a lunchtime staple for many Westmoreland County students. Today, the citron is most commonly used in holiday fruitcakes.

A woman for all seasons and a true inspiration for many, Nellie Gaskins for decades has fed and nourished the physical well being of many throughout the county. She has taught by example both patience and love for all.

This is an image of Virginia Richards, who is best remembered by her classmates for having won a prize for "Ain't That Good News."

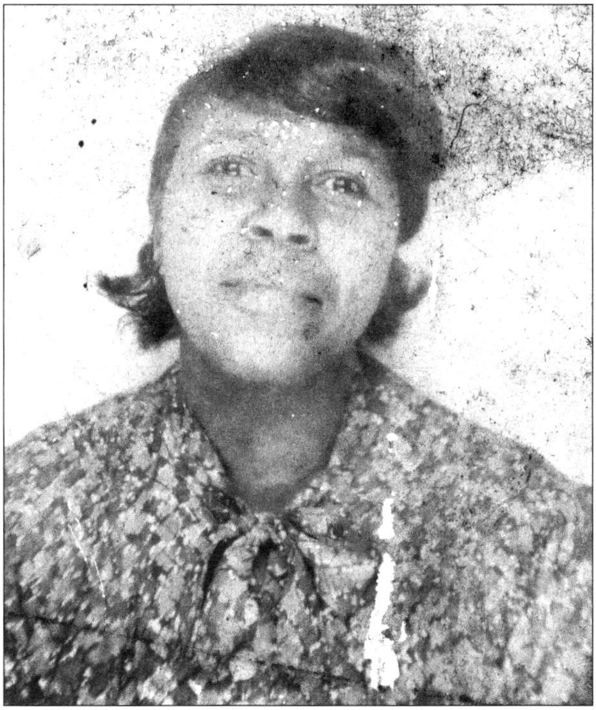

This is an image of Viola Newton, a Salem School student.

This is an image of Arlene Payne, a student from Chandler Mill Pond School.

Ethel Lomax started teaching in 1914 in Westmoreland County for $20 per month. She taught in four different schools, and by the time she retired, she had devoted 47 years to teaching.

The Power of Song

Because many of the school buildings served as churches and many of the schoolteachers also acted as Sunday school instructors, church and state mingled in the classrooms. Teachers, many times without the resource of textbooks, relied on more creative approaches, such as songs, to teach the children lessons and values. The following are two examples of songs enjoyed by students and teachers in Westmoreland County's one-room schoolhouses.

"Walk in Jerusalem"
A traditional Negro spiritual
(Courtesy of Reverend William B. Scott)
This song was said to be Julius Rosenwald's favorite song.

Chorus
    I want to be ready, I want to be ready, I want to be ready
    To walk in Jerusalem, jus like John

verse #1
    Oh John, Oh John now didn't you say walk in Jerusalem, Just like John
    That you would be there on that great day,
    Walk in Jerusalem jus like John

verse # 2
    Never been to heaven, but I've been told,
    Walk in Jerusalem just like John
    That the streets up there are paved with gold
    Walk in Jerusalem jus like John

verse #3
    Sometimes I'm up sometimes I'm down
    Walk in Jerusalem just like John
    Sometimes I'm almost level to the ground
    Walk in Jerusalem jus like John

verse # 4
    When Peter was preachin at Pentecost
    He was endowed with the Holy Ghost

verse #5
    Jesus told Thomas, said I am the man,
    See these nail prints on my hand

"Ain't-Dat Good News?"
A traditional Negro spiritual
(Courtesy of Reverend William B. Scott)

Chorus
    I'm a-goin 'to lay down this world, Goin' to shoulder up my cross,
    Goin' to take it home to my Jesus, ain't-a that good news?

verse #1
    I got a crown up in-a the King-dom, ain't-a that good news?
    I got a crown up in-a the King-dom, ain't-a that good news?

verse #2
    I got a harp up in-a the King-dom, ain't-a that good news?
    I got a harp up in-a the King-dom, ain't a that good news?

verse #3
    I got a robe up in-a the King-dom, ain't-a that good news?
    I got a robe up in-a the King-dom, ain't- a that good news?

verse #4
    I got a slip-pers in-a the King-dom, ain't a that good news?
    I got a slip-pers in-a the King-dom, ain't-a that good news?

verse #5
    I got a Sav-ior in-a the King-dom, ain't-a that good news ?
    I got a Sav-ior in-a the King-dom, ain't-a that good news?

Mudbridge School Song
(Written by Donal Thompson)

Mudbridge School by the Side of the Road
Grey paint on the weatherboard.

How long has it been there?
No one knows the little grey
School with a little red door.

Everyday we go the the little school
Whether its' warm or whether it's cool.

Glory to it's dear old name,
We hope to someday bring you fame.

Dear old Mudbridge,
Our heart will always claim.

Chandler Mill Pond School
(Mrs. Ardel Hoban had her class sing this tune at the end of each day.)

Now the day is over,
Night is drawing nigh,
Shadows of the evening
Steal across the sky.

"Equipment"
(A poem written by Beulah Smith Lewis, a student at Mudbridge)

Figure it out for yourself my lad
You've all that the greatest of men have had
Two arms, two legs, two hands, two eyes, and a brain to use if it would be wise
So with these equipments they all began
So start from the top and say I can.

Look them over the wise and grit they take their food from a common plate
With similar knives and forks they use
With similar laces they tie their shoes
This world considers them brave and smart.

But you've all they've had when they made their start
You can triumph and come to skill
You can be grit if you only will
You are well equipped for what fight you choose
And the man who has risen great deeds to do
Began his life with no more than you.

You are the handicap you must face
You are the one who must choose your place
You must say where you want to go
How much you have studied the truth to know
God has equipped you for life
But he lets you decide what you want to be

Courage must come from the soul within
Man must furnish the will to win
So figure it out for yourself my Lad
You've all that the greatest of men have had
So with these equipments they all began
So start from the top and say I can.

"When Malindy Sings"
(Written by Paul Dunbar; courtesy of Edna Jenkins Jones)

Verse I
Go' waydah, and quit dat noise Miss Lucy
Put dat music book away
What's de use of keep on trying?
If you practice til you're gray.
You can't start de notes a-flying,
Lar de ones dat ranks and rings
From de kitchen to de big woods
When Malindy sings.

Verse II
You ain't got de natural organ,
For to make the sound comes right
You ain't got these tunes and de twisting
For to make it sweet and light.
Tell you one thing now, Miss Lucy,
And I'm telling you for true
When it comes to real right singing
T'aint no easy thing to do.

Verse III
Easy 'nough for folks to hollah,
Looking at the lines and dots,
When Aah ain't no one can sing it
And the tune comes in, in spots.
But for real melodies music
Dat jest strikes your heart and clings
Jes' you stand and listen wif me
Wehn Malindy sings.

Verse IV
Ain't you never heard Malindy?
Blessed soul take up the cross
Look ahead, ain't you joking, honey?
Well you don't know what you lost.
You ought to heah dat Gal a-singing,
Robin, larks, and all de things.
Hush, dah mouths and hide da faces
When Malindy sings.

Verse V
Fiddling man, jes stops his fiddling,
Lay his fiddle on the shelf
Mockingbirds quits trying to whistle,
Cause he's jes so shamed himself
Folk a playing on the banjo,
Drops their fingers on the strings
Bless your soul forgets to move them
When Malindy sings.

Verse VI
She jest spreads her mouth and holleahs,
Come to Jesus, I will you heah,
Sinners trembling steps and voices
Timid like a drawing neah
Den she turns to rocks of ages
Simply to the cross she clings
And you find your tears a-dropping
When Malindy sings.

Verse VII
Who dat say that humble praises?
Which the master never counts
Hush you move I heah dat music,
As it rises up and mounts
Floating by the hills and valleys
Way above this burning sod
To the very Gates of God.

Verse VIII
Oh! Its sweeter than the music,
Of an educated band.
Song of Triumph in the Land.
Streams holier than evening
When the . . . church bells ring
As I sit and calmly listen
When Malindy sings.

Verse IX
Tousah, stop that banking, hear me?
Malindy make that child keep still
Can't you heah dem echoes calling?
From the valleys to the hills.
Let me listen, I can heah it,
Through the brush of angels' wings
Soft and sweet Swing low sweet
Chariots, coming for to carry me home,
Swing low sweet chariot, coming for
to carry me home, as Malindy sings.

"Myself"
(Written by Edgar A. Guest; courtesy of Sebbie Jenkins)

I have to live with myself, and so
I want to be fit for myself to know,
I want to be able, as days go by,
Always to look myself straight in the eye;
I don't want to stand, with the setting sun,
And hate myself for things I have done.

I don't want to keep on a closet shelf
A lot of secrets about myself,
And fool myself, as I come and go,
Into thinking that nobody else will know
The kind of a man I really am;
I don't want to dress yp myself in sham

I want to go out with my head erect,
I want to deserve all men's respect;
But here in the struggle for fame and pelf
I want to be able to like myself.
I don't want to look at myself and know
That I'm bluster and bluff and empty show.

I can never hide myself from me;
I see what others may never see;
I know what others may never know,
I never can fool myself and so,
Whatever happens, I want to be
Self-respecting and conscience free.

"Build a Better World"
(Written by an unknown Templemans student)

"Build a better world," said God
and I answered,
"How? The world is such a vast place,
and so complicated now,
And I am small and useless;
There's nothing I can do."
But God, in all His wisdom said,
"Just build a better you."

ONE AND TWO-ROOM SCHOOLHOUSES
(1870–1958)

NAME	LOCATION	CURRENT POST OFFICE
First Colonial Beach School Elementary	Jackson Street (sold 1942)	Colonial Beach
Second Colonial Beach Elementary	Lincoln Avenue	Colonial Beach
Headfield	New Monrovia Road	Potomac Beach
Monroe Hall No. 6	Jame Monroe Highway	Colonial Beach
Jefferson	James Monroe Highway	Colonial Beach
Robs Hill	Leedstown Road	Leedstown / Colonial Beach
Oak Grove	Parrish Lane	Colonial Beach
Gravel Run	Kings Highway	Potomac Mills / Colonial Beach
Eltham	Macedonia Road	Maple Grove / Colonial Beach
New Richmond	Grants Hill Church Road	Colonial Beach
Sugarland	Flat Iron Road	Foneswood
George Washington	Kings Highway	Potomac Mills / Colonial Beach
Sweet Home	Crookhorn Road	Montross
Morning Star	Zacata Road	Hinnom / Montross
First Zacata School	George Reeds Farm 3200 Block Zacata Road	Zacata
Second Zacata School	2638 Zacata Road	Montross
Third Zacata School	Zacata Road (across from Siloam Church)	Zacata / Montross
Fourth Zacata School	Zacata Road (across from Siloam Church)	Zacata / Montross
First Chandler Mill Pond	Dingley Road	Montross
Second Chandler Mill Pond	Dingley Road	Montross

ONE AND TWO-ROOM SCHOOLHOUSES
(CONTINUED)

NAME	LOCATION	CURRENT POST OFFICE
Templemans	3984 Neenah Road	Templemans / Montross
First Galilee (by the church)	Kings Highway	Montross
Second Galilee (in the Odd Fellows Hall)	Kings Highway	Montross
First Erica School	Mount Holly Road and Glebe Road	Montross
Second Erica School	Erica Road	Montross
First Frog Hall	Sandy Point Road	Saindy Point
Second Frog Hall	Sandy Point Road	Sandy Point
First Mudbridge School	Colespoint Road	Colespoint
Second Mudbridge School (former Coles Point white school)	Colespoint and Parham Roads	Colespoint
First Hacketts Hill	Kings Mill Road	Hackets Hill / Kinsale
Second Hacketts Hill	Kings Mill Road	Hackets Hill / Kinsale
Bethsaida	Sandy Point Road	Sandy Point
Potomac	Nomini Hall Road	Hague
First Kremlin	Antioch Road	Kremlin
Second Kremlin	Antioch Road	Kremlin / Oldhams
Salem	Erica Road	Upper Matchotic / Mount Holly
First Zion	Zion Church Road	Tucker Hill / Kinsale
Second Zion	Rose Tucker Road	Tucker Hill / Kinsale
Zion Auxiliary Space (Odd Fellows Hall)	Rose Tucker Road	Tucker Hill / Kinsale

A History of Leadership

Much credit for the progress of the public school system in Westmoreland County has been due to the vision and labors of its superintendents of schools. The following names detail the superintendents who have filled this office:

Reverend William W. Walker	1871–1873
Colonel Thomas Brown	1873–1877
Willoughby Newton Brown	1877–1878
Reverend Wilbur F. Davis	1878–1882
Reverend H.H. Fones	1882–1886
T. Hunter Jr.	1886–1905
Thomas Brown	1905–1909
George W. Murphy	1909–1913
Blake T. Newton	1913–1954
Robert T. Ryland	1954–1965
James V. Law	1965–1969
C.B. Chandler	1969–1972
S.M. Haga	1972–1975
Charles L. Pierce Sr.	1975–1992
Dr. Larry Hixson	1992–1999

Closing Words

Westmoreland County's proud traditions in education and improvement ring true in this oft-spoken phrase by Mrs. Campbell:

> GOOD, BETTER, BEST
> NEVER LET IT REST
> UNTIL THE GOOD GETS BETTER
> AND THE BETTER GETS BEST.